MW01601414

THE TWEEN COMMANDMENTS

GOD'S SPECIAL GIFT

By Norina Purro

Contact the author Norina Purro at:
https://books.by/the-tween-commandments
forhisglory737@gmail.com

Second Paperback Edition November 2025.

Edited by Norina Purro & Cindy Panek
Cover art by Nina Urcavich
Layout by Cindy Panek
Images by Norina Purro

PAPER BACK
ISBN 979-8-9999683-1-9

DEDICATION

I, Norina, dedicate this book to God, the Creator of all things. I cherish His wisdom and knowledge as He guides me through life. I pray His will be carried out in my life from here to eternity.

Matthew 6:10 NKJV Your kingdom come. Your will be done on earth as it is in heaven.

In love, I dedicate this book to my children, Anthony, Nina, Ben, Sandi, Robert, Norina J, John, Jorel, and my grandchildren: Noah, Jordan, Josie, Ella, Nitalya, Jeremiah, Micah, Sebastian, Hailey, Robert Jr., Peyton, and Quinn.

Psalms 127:3 NKJV Behold, children are a heritage from the Lord, The fruit of the womb is a reward.   (From God)

Proverbs 17:6 NKJV Children's children are the crown of old men, And the glory of children is their father.

ACKNOWLEDGEMENTS

I would like to express my sincere gratitude to the individuals who provided invaluable support and encouragement throughout the creation of this book.

First, thank you to **Ben and Nina Urcavich** for generously providing a quiet space for me to work. Your love for me and your unwavering commitment to God have been a true source of inspiration.

I am deeply grateful to **Pastor Norman Wise** and **Tye Riter** for their guidance in presenting the Ten Commandments. Their formal training in Christian theology was a great help. Thank you, Josh Hall, for the encouragement.

A special thanks to **Debra Cusick** for sharing her time and wisdom. Her skills as an English teacher were essential in the editing process.

To **William Hoppe**, thank you for diligently reviewing the manuscript and identifying errors that needed correction.

I would also like to acknowledge my friend **Samantha Azure** for her excellent editing skills and valuable input.

Finally, I would like to extend a very special thank you to my dear friend, **Cindy Panek**. Her patience, timeless effort, and technical expertise were critical in preparing this book for printing and navigating the publishing process.

PREFACE

To the parents, teachers, pastors, and youth leaders, the Ten Commandments, often perceived as a set of rigid rules, are in actuality a loving guide from God to help us live joyful and meaningful lives. This book aims to present these fundamental principles in a way that is both engaging and accessible for young readers. Children are naturally receptive to moral guidance when presented through captivating stories and relatable characters. Instead of employing a dry or overly didactic approach, I have chosen to narrate the Commandments through exciting tales that capture tweens' imaginations while subtly imparting important moral and ethical lessons. Each story is carefully crafted to illustrate a specific commandment, allowing tween-age children to learn through experiences and emotional engagement rather than abstract concepts. The colorful and dynamic illustrations further enhance the storytelling, making the learning process visually stimulating and enjoyable. I hope that this book will not merely convey factual information but will cultivate a deeper understanding of the principles behind the Ten Commandments, empowering tweens to make conscious ethical choices and to build stronger relationships with God, themselves, and others.

I believe that faith should be a journey of discovery, filled with joy, wonder, and a sense of belonging. I invite young readers to embark on this exciting exploration, to discover the wisdom within the Ten Commandments, and to find inspiration in the countless ways God's love is expressed. May this book serve as a cherished companion on the path toward spiritual growth, offering guidance and support in cultivating a strong moral compass.

THE TWEEN COMMANDMENTS
TABLE OF CONTENTS

THE BRIDE OF CHRIST

Matthew 25 NKJV 1"Then the kingdom of heaven shall be likened to ten virgins who took their lamps and went out to meet the bridegroom. 2Now five of them were wise, and five were foolish. 3Those who were foolish took their lamps and took no oil with them, 4but the wise took oil in their vessels with their lamps. 5But while the bridegroom was delayed, they all slumbered and slept.

6"And at midnight a cry was heard: 'Behold, the bridegroom is coming; go out to meet him!' 7Then all those virgins arose and trimmed their lamps. 8And the foolish said to the wise, 'Give us some of your oil, for our lamps are going out.' 9But the wise answered, saying, 'No, lest there should not be enough for us and you; but go rather to those who sell, and buy for yourselves.' 10And while they went to buy, the bridegroom came, and those who were ready went in with him to the wedding; and the door was shut.

1

11"Afterward the other virgins came also, saying, 'Lord, Lord, open to us!' 12But he answered and said, 'Assuredly, I say to you, I do not know you.'13"Watch therefore, for you know neither the day nor the hour in which the Son of Man is coming.

JOHN 14:21 NKJV 21He who has My commandments and keeps them, it is he who loves Me. And he who loves Me will be loved by My Father, and I will love him and manifest Myself to him."

Matthew 22:37-40 NKJV Jesus said to him, "You shall love the LORD your God with all your heart, with all your soul, and with all your mind.'
And the second is like it: 'You shall love your neighbor as yourself.' On these two commandments hang all the Law and the Prophets."

Loving others is very important. The church is the body of Christ, and we need to stick together and love each other.

2

I remember when my grandma first told me about the "spotless bride." She explained that it was like a really, really special wedding, where the bride was perfect, and that's how Jesus wants His Church to be, all clean and shiny.

In the Bible, Jesus says that He is going to meet His bride in the clouds. The spotless bride is like getting ready for the biggest party ever, and everyone wants to look their best.

The Bible describes the Church as a bride. Not just any bride, though, but a super special one, all perfect and clean with no yucky spots or wrinkles, just totally good and perfect. The spotless bride is continually being changed and cleaned up by the Holy Spirit, ultimately to be presented to Jesus as a spotless bride.

When the wedding preparations truly began, it wasn't just about the sparkly dress, though that was quite important. The dress, you see, is special. It was being fixed up, smoothed, and polished, as if it were alive, always becoming more and more perfect. This ongoing work, this careful cleaning and perfecting, was preparing the spotless bride for her groom. It was a constant process of becoming more beautiful and pure for the special day. This is called sanctification.

3

And then there was the promise. The bride wasn't just getting a fancy dress; she was making a big promise. She was going to be completely faithful to her groom. It's like when you promise your best friend you'll always share your toys, no matter what. The Church, just like the bride, is called to be faithful too. My grandma once said that being too friendly with everything going on in the world can make you not so friendly with God. So, it's important to choose who you're faithful to.

This preparation wasn't just about looking good or making promises; it was also about growing. The Church is encouraged to get stronger and know more. It's like when you learn new things in school or get better at playing a game. This spiritual growth means learning more about faith and becoming wiser by studying your Bible. It's a journey, and the spotless bride, through all this transforming, purifying, and faithfulness, is constantly becoming more ready.

4

I remembered what the book of James said about faith without works being dead. It wasn't enough to just think I believed in Jesus; my belief needed to do something. I started noticing things differently. If someone dropped their books, I'd pick them up. If a friend looked sad, I'd try to make them smile, even if it was just with a goofy face. This wasn't about getting a sticker or a gold star; it was about my faith being alive, showing that I wanted to be like Jesus and help people.

James 2:14-17
14What does it profit, my brethren, if someone says he has faith but does not have works? Can faith save him? 15If a brother or sister is naked and destitute of daily food, 16and one of you says to them, "Depart in peace, be warmed and filled," but you do not give them the things which are needed for the body, what does it profit? 17Thus also faith by itself, if it does not have works, is dead.

Later that week, I was walking home from school, my backpack feeling heavier than usual. Ahead of me, I saw a girl sitting by herself on a park bench. Her shoulders were slumped, and she was staring at her shoes. My first thought was to just keep walking, to get home and have a snack. But then, the words about faith doing something echoed in my head. I thought about how I would feel if I were her, all alone and sad. I found myself walking towards the bench. It felt a little strange. Then, it was like a little nudge. I stopped. It wasn't a big, dramatic thing, just a pause. I looked at her again, and even though I didn't know her story, I remembered my own belief that being kind is important. So, I walked over to the bench, sat down, and asked, "Are you okay?" My voice sounded a little squeaky, even to me.

5

She looked up, and her eyes were red. I didn't have any special words, but I sat there and just waited. It felt like a choice, like the kind of choice the Bible talks about, where your belief makes you want to do something, not just think about it.

We sat there for a bit, and then she mumbled something about losing her dog. I didn't have a dog to offer, but I did have a spare granola bar in my backpack that I'd been saving. I pulled it out and offered it to her. It wasn't a grand gesture, but it was something. She took it, and a tiny smile flickered on her face. It made me feel like my faith, the kind that James talks about, was actually alive.

This wasn't just about looking good or making promises; it was also about growing. The Church is encouraged to get stronger and know more. It's like when you learn new things in school or get better at playing a game. This spiritual growth means learning more about faith and becoming wiser, studying your bible. It's a journey, and the spotless bride, through all this growing, purifying, and faithfulness, is always becoming more ready.

6

To be the perfect bride, we must live holy lives set apart from sin. I remember learning about how we should live in a way that shows we are special and different from the world. This meant not doing wrong things, like being greedy for toys or treats, or saying unkind words that could hurt others. It was about choosing to be good, even when it is hard. I thought about how sometimes I wanted to keep all the best snacks for myself, but then I remembered that sharing was a better way to be.

So, I started paying closer attention to my choices. When I saw some kids wanting to play a game that seemed a bit unfair, I chose not to join in. Instead, I found a group playing tag, and we ran and laughed, enjoying the sunshine and the fun of the game. It felt good to make a choice that felt clean and bright inside. I learned to choose kindness and honesty, and to be happy with who I am and what I have.

I remember my Grandma explaining it this way: being set apart, sanctified, and holy means I've grown closer to Jesus, like a special friend who has dedicated their life to Him. When we take Holy Communion, it's like renewing a special promise, almost like a wedding vow, to Jesus.

She said that just as a bride must stay faithful by not doing things that would upset her future husband, we, the bride, have to remain separate from the ways of the world. It's about being faithful because the whole church is promised to Jesus, but she also sadly mentioned that not everyone will be at the big wedding feast. People in the church who are unfaithful to that special promise won't meet Jesus in the clouds. Jesus is coming for His spotless bride in the clouds. The body still belongs to Him; He saved them on the cross, but they still need more sanctification.

So, I try my best to be watchful and pray. Grandma always reminded me to pray that I would be found worthy, just like it says in Luke.

Luke 21:36. 34"But take heed to yourselves, lest your hearts be weighed down with carousing, drunkenness, and cares of this life, and that Day come on you unexpectedly. 35 For it will come as a snare on all those who dwell on the face of the whole earth. 36 Watch therefore, and pray always that you may be counted worthy to escape all these things that will come to pass, and to stand before the Son of Man."

It's not about being perfect all the time, but about trying to live in a way that shows Jesus how much I love Him and want to be His faithful friend. I think about how much it means to be chosen and set apart for something so important. It's like being given a special job that only I can do, and I want to do it well.

My grandma explained that the Church is like a big family of people who believe in God. However, even though everyone may be part of the family, not everyone always acts as if they're truly following God's calling. Some people might be in church because it is a tradition, or they don't understand what God wants from them. So, it's kind of like some people are really living out that calling, and others are still figuring it out. The ones that are still figuring it out are the ones that will not meet Jesus in the clouds unless they get right with God.

Grandma used the big word, ecclesia, and said it means the called-out ones, the ones who left the crowd. It's like a special group, a remnant, that's set apart for God alone. My heart felt a strange tug as I heard those words, "the bride will be taken out of the group who claim to be Christians, because not all Christians are really ready. Some don't believe with all their hearts, souls, and minds." It sounded like a secret mission, like some of us were chosen for something special, something separate from everyone else.

9

This made me think about how some people live. Grandma said that if believers keep living like everyone else in the world, doing things that aren't what Jesus would want, they won't be ready for Him when He comes back. It's like if you're going on a special trip, you wouldn't pack your regular school clothes, right? You'd pack something special.

She explained that all true believers in Jesus are "spiritual believers" in Christ. This idea of spiritual idolatry stuck with me. It means God wouldn't marry His bride if she had anything in her life that took the place of Him. This can be a person, such as a mom, dad, sister, brother, daughter, son, girlfriend, boyfriend, or anyone more important than God.

Spiritual Idolatry is wanting too many toys, or caring about things we own more than God. It can also be certain beliefs, or even activities that we make more important than Him. If we honestly seek God in prayer and spend less time with these things, it will be easy to get rid of "Spiritual Idols".

10

So, I realized that being part of the called-out ones means more than just saying you believe. It means living a life that shows you're ready for Jesus. It's like practicing for a big soccer game. You have to train, eat well, and follow the coach's rules. If you don't, you won't be in top shape when it's time to play.

I started to wonder if I was truly living as a spiritual believer, or if there were other gods in my heart that I needed to let go of. It felt like a big responsibility but also exciting, like being part of a secret, important plan.

This feeling makes me want to be more careful about my choices, like choosing what I do on the internet, games I play, and what I watch on TV. Thinking about who I spend my time with. I want to be a good example, and I know that staying close to Jesus helps me do that. The Holy Spirit helps me to change how I act. It's like getting a superpower that makes me want to be better. It's the same with faith; when we walk with Christ, our light shines, and people can see that we are different.

11

The thought of that wedding day keeps me focused, and I want to be ready, dressed in my best spiritual clothes, my spotless bride gown, prepared to celebrate with Jesus. It's a big adventure, and I'm learning every day how to be a better bride for my Savior.

12

THE T*WE*EN COMMANDMENTS
INTRODUCTION

Imagine a world overflowing with kindness, honesty, and respect, which is what God truly wishes for us. The Ten Commandments provide a loving path to a peaceful and joyful life, guiding us through our journey. The Ten Commandments are not troublesome rules. God created a way for us to live out of love, rather than harsh rules. The Ten Commandments protect us. They are a loving guide that keeps us safe.

These commandments help us to choose good over evil. We should choose kindness over selfishness, truth over deceit, and love over hate. When we make these choices, we receive benefits and create a brighter world.

15

Lily decided to be honest after she found a five-dollar bill. The happiness she felt upon returning the money to its grateful owner was worth more to her than what she could spend it on.

Ben helped his friend with a math problem. He could have made fun of His friend, but instead, sharing what he knew with his friend made him feel good. His friend learned how to solve the math problem.

Maya decided she would not spread rumors about her classmate and would remain a trustworthy friend. She realized that rumors can hurt people and destroy friendships.

16

The actions of young people like Lily, Ben, and Maya show us that even young people have the power to change the world through their good choices. Tweens can be blessed by choosing kindness, truthfulness, and love, even when they are facing tough situations.

Sam and his brother were fighting. Sam decided to stop arguing over video games and talk to his brother with respect. The happiness they experienced while playing video games helped them understand how God's word leads to joy.

Following these commandments isn't always easy. Sometimes we will make mistakes. And that's okay! God understands that we're not perfect. God expects us to try to live by the Ten Commandments while being ready to ask for forgiveness. When we fail, God will forgive us for our sins. The goal isn't perfection but growing by doing the right thing. At the same time, we are learning from our mistakes and serving as a light for God's kingdom. Jesus loves us unconditionally, which means He loves us even if we make mistakes. God is always with us to help us.

17

God loves us so much that He became a human just for us. He was beaten and died on the cross to pay for our sins. The blood that He shed on the cross erases our sins as if our sins were never there. God is holy and hates sin. He forgave us so we could be with Him in heaven forever.

He wants us in heaven because He loves us and wants a relationship with us.

After He was hung on the cross, Jesus went back up to heaven, on the third day, and overcame death for all who believe in Him. Now He sits in glory beside the Father. He promises that He will return so everyone can see how beautiful He is when He returns to earth.

Our relationship with Jesus depends completely on His grace. When He was on the earth, He never sinned. He died for us on the cross so that we could be with Him in heaven. He sent the Holy Spirit to guide us and make it possible for us to show God how much we love Him. The Holy Spirit guides, strengthens, and comforts us.

The Ten Commandments are more than rules; they are a way for us to live through love and compassion. We learn that love and compassion lead to joy and a better relationship with God and the people He created. These commandments teach us the importance of kindness and respect. When we care for others, we find happiness through making others smile. God's Ten Commandments are a guide for us to learn to be like Him. He is a loving God and Father.

Obeying the Ten Commandments does not mean we earn God's love because he already loves us without conditions. By living God's way, we show His love in the way we think and the way we act, as well as the things we say. We show our love through our decisions to act kindly, to remain truthful, and to show respect to others. The Ten Commandments teach us that true happiness comes from having peace, rather than material things.

Living the way God wants us to, doing the right thing, and working to improve the world brings us true peace. Following God's commandments leads to true joy, which fills our hearts with peace in every part of our lives.

The Ten Commandments are a guiding light that enables us to make wise decisions in our lives. These commandments represent blessings rather than burdens. God's special gift to us helps us achieve happiness and fulfillment while providing constant protection through His love and care.

God wants us to love others as we love ourselves. Choosing to share isn't always easy. Although sharing feels like losing something precious to us, the joy of seeing another person happy when we share often becomes greater than our desire to keep things to ourselves. When we make the decision to share, we create happiness in others, and at the same time, it brings us closer to them. Many of God's commandments teach us that He wants us to love, show compassion, and be generous. Doing the right thing requires both effort and self-discipline.

The Ten Commandments work as a necessary guide to building a powerful and loving connection with God. Jesus is our best friend who provides the greatest love and support throughout our lives.

The first four commandments show us that "You shall love the Lord your God with all your heart, with all your soul, and with all your strength." Jesus Christ called this the great commandment. Jesus set the example of putting God first.

The last six commandments are all about being respectful and responsible towards others. God wants us to love others as we love ourselves. No cheating, stealing, lying, or being jealous; it's all about choosing to be kind, honest, and respectful. What we do affects everyone around us, including our families, friends, and our entire community. A world without gossip, jealousy, and dishonesty would be a much more awesome place, one full of kindness, trust, and love. That's the kind of world we should all try to create.

CHAPTER 1
THE FIRST COMMANDMENT

Exodus 20:1-3 And God spoke all these words, saying:
2"I am the Lord your God, who brought you out of the land of Egypt, out of the house of bondage. 3"You shall have no other gods before Me.

The First Commandment is, "You shall have no other gods before Me". This commandment tells us to put God first. As we learn more about God's commandments, we learn that they are not just rules, but a way to bring happiness and peace to ourselves and those around us. God's values reflect His nature. He wants us to live by choosing His values in our lives.

With the first commandment, we are taught to have no other gods before the one and only true God. To us, this means understanding that God should be the most important thing in our lives. It's like thinking of Him as our number one person, just as our earthly parents are number one.

Our best friend is always there for us. A true friend knows how to make us laugh, even when we are having a total meltdown over a bad grade or other bad things that happen in our lives. God is the ultimate best friend! Our relationship with God goes beyond sharing fun moments with friends and video gaming activities. As we enjoy time with our friends, we feel God's presence as He cheers us on.

When God comes first in our hearts and minds, we are being loyal and faithful to Him, just as we are to our best friend. We know that when we put God first, everything else falls into place. It's like when we build a sand castle, He is there with us. This commandment is a reminder that God is always with us, He helps us, and we can trust and rely on Him. There is no other god that can do that because no other god is living and real.

23

This also helps us understand the importance of worshipping the one true God only. It's about knowing the one true God, who created everything, and loving Him above all else. This commandment is like a light, guiding us towards a deeper relationship with God and helping us stay on the right path.

24

CHAPTER 2
THE SECOND COMMANDMENT

Exodus 20:4-6: "You shall not make for yourself a carved image—any likeness of anything that is in heaven above, or that is in the earth beneath, or that is in the water under the earth; you shall not bow down to them nor serve them. For I, the Lord your God, am a jealous God, visiting the iniquity of the fathers upon the children to the third and fourth generations of those who hate Me, but showing mercy to thousands, to those who love Me and keep My commandments."

The second commandment teaches against idolatry, placing anything above God. Video games can become a "false god"! It is easy to get distracted by them. My friend Alex missed his little sister's birthday party because he was trying to beat a level. That's, like, a total bummer for his sister, and seriously, is a video game really that important? A video game can't hug you back or anything.

God wants to be first in our lives. It's like having a super awesome, powerful friend who you really appreciate. Being a good person, like showing kindness and being honest, is the only way to really show that you respect God. It's not about being scared of Him, it's about being thankful for everything good. Jesus wants us to behave like Him. He loves us deeply, and so we should love Him with all our hearts and love others. He created all people, and He loves them.

Some examples of things we can easily put before God are people, family, things that we own, like toys, television, houses, cars, clothes, makeup, self-image, soccer, football, a job, money, having fun, and even food. He wants us to eat, but He doesn't want us to make food the most important thing in our lives. God wants to be the most important thing in our life. These are only a few things to show us that anything that we put before God can become an idol.

Whatever we love more than God is putting other gods before Him, the one and only true God.

CHAPTER 3
THE THIRD COMMANDMENT

Exodus 20:7: "You shall not take the name of the Lord your God in vain, for the Lord will not hold him guiltless who takes His name in vain."

This part about God's name is kinda serious. My grandpa always says we shouldn't use God's name in vain, and that makes sense. We must not disrespect God. If someone you respect keeps getting their name thrown around carelessly, you would feel bad about it. God deserves way more respect than that. He made everything, after all! That's way cooler than any video game.

Yeah, so like, it's not just yelling "Oh my God!" Or writing "OMG" all the time, even though that's totally annoying. It's also when you say, "God made me do it!" after you've done something wrong, like when I accidentally broke my mom's favorite vase. Oops! That's totally blaming God, and that's not right. It's also, like, using His name in jokes that aren't funny, you know? Like, making fun of what He stands for. That's just disrespectful.

31

CHAPTER 4
THE FOURTH COMMANDMENT

Exodus 20:8-11 "Remember the Sabbath day, to keep it holy. Six days you shall labor and do all your work, but the seventh day is the Sabbath of the Lord your God. In it you shall do no work: you, nor your son, nor your daughter, nor your male servant, nor your female servant, nor your cattle, nor your stranger who is within your gates. For in six days the Lord made the heavens and the earth, the sea, and all that is in them, and rested the seventh day. Therefore, the Lord blessed the Sabbath day and hallowed it."

As you can see, God rested on the seventh day. He wants us to have a time of rest. God wants us to take a break on the Lord's Day. We need to chill out, or we will totally crash. Except this is way more important because it's about God. It's not just a day off from school and homework; it's about spending time with my family, attending church, and simply being quiet. We can spend time thinking about all the awesome things God made, like the sunset or my puppy, Sparky.

It's supposed to be fun, not a punishment! Some people make it a drag, but it doesn't have to be that way. We could have a special family breakfast, go for a bike ride, or even do a crazy puzzle together. It's about recharging our batteries. You know! So we aren't all stressed and grumpy the rest of the week. And it helps us remember that even God took a break after making everything! That all about showing God we love Him, not just saying it.

Genesis 2:2-3 NKJV
2 And on the seventh day God ended His work which He had done, and He rested on the seventh day from all His work which He had done. 3 Then God blessed the seventh day and sanctified it.

33

Church is essential, singing songs are fun, and praying makes us feel at peace. It's like having a secret, special date with God, a whole day just for Him! It's not just church stuff. I love looking at nature, the way the sun shines through the leaves, or how fluffy the clouds are. That's worshipping God, too, right? We can enjoy reading our Bible; some stories are seriously amazing! And thinking about how awesome God is, well, that's pretty awesome too.

Observing the Sabbath is different. Sometimes it's relaxing, like when we all just hang out and read books. Other times, it's really quiet, but it's important. It's a time to think about how awesome God is and how blessed we are to have our family. When we spend time alone with God, this brings us closer to Jesus, even when we pray alone before bed.

It's a time to say thank you for everything good, such as our friends, family, and even our pets. It's about remembering Jesus and how much He loves us. It's also super cool to think that we are all connected, like one big church family, even if we argue sometimes. God made people all over the world different, with different ways of living. This makes life way more interesting!

CHAPTER 5
THE FIFTH COMMANDMENT

Exodus 20:12: "Honor your father and your mother, that your days may be long upon the land which the Lord your God is giving you."

The fifth commandment, "Honor your father and your mother," is very important! It's not about being a total robot and doing everything they say without even thinking. Still, it's about showing them we appreciate all the things they do.

Our parents? They're our personal driver! They drive us to school, soccer, and even to hang out with friends; they're always driving us around. And food?

Warm bed? Always! Even when we're being a total pain in the neck. They taught us everything from eating to sleeping, walking, talking, and even sharing.

Honoring our parents is about listening to them, even when their advice on homework or who we hang out with seems totally old-fashioned. They've been there, done that; they were young once, too. And the whole online safety thing is annoying to hear about constantly, but actually quite important. Really important! Think about it, they're just trying to keep us safe from creeps and stuff.

Showing them how much we appreciate them means helping with chores, even the boring ones, like doing the dishes or taking out the trash. Little things can make a big difference, like chatting with them about our day and saying thank you a lot. You can do something thoughtful, like making them a card or their favorite snack.

Just listen when they talk; it means a lot to them. A simple "thanks" goes a long way. Offer to help with errands or run to the store. Spending time with them, talking, and hearing their stories shows we care. It's about listening to them, even when you think they're totally wrong. It's about understanding that they're just people, too, trying their best, even when they make mistakes sometimes. It's about respecting their opinions, even if they're different from yours. Basically, be patient and kind; they love us a lot.

Being a tween is all about wanting to be independent, to have our own freedom, and to make our own choices. Our parents are helping us to become independent, and hopefully dependent on God.
This goes for grandparents, aunts, uncles, and other older family members, too. They've got so many fun stories and so much wisdom. Listen to them, ask questions, they've lived through so much! Learning from their experiences is awesome. They've been through the ups and downs of life, and they can teach us many things.

Our grandpas might teach us how to fix a bike, or build a birdhouse, or show us their awesome secret fishing spot. Learning from them is awesome, and it brings us closer as a family. Everyone in our family is special, even the weird uncles and crazy cousins! Making them happy makes us happy, too. It's like a secret superpower of happiness!"

Have we ever had a fight with our brother or sister? Or maybe we messed up and feel bad about it? Forgiving them and yourself is super important for a happy family. It's like letting go of a heavy backpack full of anger. Holding onto that anger will only make us feel worse, and it hurts our relationship with them. Forgiveness isn't saying what they did was okay; it's about choosing to feel better and move on. Think of it as giving ourselves a break.

Maybe they've done things that upset you. Forgiveness helps everyone heal and makes things way better. This helps everyone in the family feel closer and more loved. Honoring our parents and family is about building strong, healthy relationships based on respect and love. It's about learning from their experience and making them feel good.

This goes for our parents, too. It's all about talking things out, telling them how we feel, but without being a total jerk. We need to think before we speak! Our words can either make things better or way worse, so choose wisely. If we are mad, say it calmly, not by yelling or throwing a fit. Don't blame them for everything; we need to just explain what's bugging us. Try to see things from their point of view; they might have good reasons for what they do.

Saying prayers together is a great way to feel closer to God and one another. It doesn't have to be super long or formal; even a quick "thank you" for the food or a prayer for a friend can make a difference. You could take turns leading the prayer, or choose a cool Bible verse to read aloud. It's like a secret code for showing we care about our family and God.

Hanging out with our family is super important! It's way more than just eating dinner together; it's about being a team and making awesome memories. Think about all the fun we have playing games, going on trips, or just laughing together. Those are the things that really matter.

Basically, loving our family is like showing God how much we appreciate all the good things in our lives. It takes effort, but it's totally worth it! We get a stronger family, a closer relationship with God, and a whole lot of love and laughter. It's a journey, with ups and downs, but the best kind of adventure we will ever have.

Sometimes we don't have a dad or a mom or even a sister or a brother. Family isn't only about moms and dads. Family can be the people who care for you, love you, and help you grow. You are part of God's big family, and you have people who love you and want you to feel safe and happy.

I know it might be hard sometimes when we see other kids with their moms and dads, but it is important to know that we are so loved, and God is always with us. He's never going to leave us.

"God is a father to the fatherless and a defender of widows." God is watching over us as our loving parent.

Psalm 68:5, NKJV
A father of the fatherless, a defender of widows, Is God in His holy habitation.

CHAPTER 6
THE SIXTH COMMANDMENT

Exodus 20:13: "You shall not murder."

The don't murder commandment isn't just about, like, avoiding murder, right? You know, physically killing someone. It's also about being nice to yourself and everyone else. It means looking after yourself, eating healthy, getting enough sleep, and not doing things that hurt you, like getting super angry all the time or hurting yourself on purpose. It's about realizing that your life is super valuable, and so is everyone else's.

Finally, 'Don't kill' also means being kind to all living things. Think about how amazing animals are, the crazy patterns on a butterfly's wings, a dolphin leaping out of the water, or a majestic eagle soaring through the sky. They're all amazing creations, and we should treat them with respect and kindness. We need to protect them!"

45

This doesn't mean we should never hurt a bug or anything. Like, if a mosquito is buzzing around your head and trying to bite you, you totally get to swat it! Or if a huge, scary spider is crawling on you, you can definitely get rid of it. And if a dog is trying to eat your lunch, hopefully that doesn't happen; you gotta protect yourself! It's all about staying safe.

Okay, imagine this: you're playing tag at recess, and someone accidentally trips you. Even though it wasn't on purpose, it still hurt, right? That's kind of what this is about. We shouldn't hurt people, accidentally, if we can help it. And definitely not on purpose! It's like the Golden Rule: treat others as you would like to be treated. Think how sad you'd be if someone totally wrecked your awesome toy. Yeah, don't do that to anyone else!

And it's not just about avoiding scraped knees. Being mean to someone, like calling them names or spreading rumors, is also hurting them. It's like throwing a mean snowball at their heart! Think about how awful it feels when someone makes fun of you or leaves you out. Words can really sting, even worse than some bumps and bruises. So use your words to be awesome, not to be a bully! Gossiping is like spreading a contagious disease of negativity; don't be the one to start it! Let's build each other up, not tear each other down.

Jesus said, *"You have heard that it was said to those of old, 'You shall not murder; and whoever murders will be liable to judgment.' But I say to you that everyone who is angry with his brother will be liable to judgment; whoever insults his brother will be liable to the council; and whoever says, 'You fool!' will be liable to the hell of fire" (Matthew 5:21).*

CHAPTER 7
THE SEVENTH COMMANDMENT

Exodus 20:14: "You shall not commit adultery."

"You shall not commit adultery", that sounds super grown-up, right? It's basically about being totally honest and keeping your promises. Think of it like this: it's about being true to your friends, family, and yourself. If you
say you'll do something, you do it! It's about building strong relationships based on trust. Imagine having a secret code with your best friend, that's trust! Adultery breaks that secret code in a marriage; it's a huge betrayal of trust. Marriage is a really long-term promise to be the best partner you can
be. It's about two people building their lives together. Think of it like building an awesome castle. We're focusing on the building blocks of trust right now, long before marriage. Marriage is a super important, long-term commitment, like an amazing toy castle; it takes time, effort, and a lot of tiny bricks. You might want to call those bricks little acts of kindness and honesty.

49

Adultery is like someone coming along and smashing part of that castle; it's devastating.

Right now, your most important relationships are with your family and friends. Being faithful and honest with them is practicing for those bigger relationships in the future.

Here are some ways to be faithful:

1. Being faithful to a friend, if your friend shares a secret with you, you keep it! That's faithfulness.
2. Keeping your word, if you promise to help with chores, you do it. No excuses!
3. Returning borrowed items: If you borrow your brother's video game, you return it on time. No sneaking around.
4. Telling the truth even when it's tough. Maybe you accidentally broke your mom's favorite vase. Telling the truth might get you in trouble, but it shows you're responsible and that you respect her. It's way better than letting her think someone else broke it!

Being honest and faithful isn't just about avoiding trouble; it's about building stronger bonds with everyone in your life. It's about making people feel safe and cared for. It makes you a better person, a better friend, a better sibling, and it builds a foundation for a healthy and happy future, even before you think about marriage. It's all about showing love and respect in all your relationships, big and small.

The Bible, in Proverbs 12:22, says, "The LORD detests lying lips, but he delights in people who are trustworthy." God values truthfulness and integrity above all else.

James 5:12 reminds us, "Above all, my brothers and sisters, never swear, not by heaven or earth or anything else. Let your 'Yes' be yes and your, No, no, or you will be condemned."

Mathew 5:37 "Just let your 'Yes' be yes, and your 'No,' no; for anything more than these comes from the evil one."

This reinforces the importance of keeping our word, for to do otherwise is to invite negative consequences into our lives.

When we keep our promises, we are building a foundation of trust, not just with others but also with God. Think of it this way: God's word is like a huge, incredibly important promise. He always keeps His promises to us. When we try our best to keep our promises to others, we reflect His faithfulness and show the world what it means to live a life pleasing to Him. It's a way of showing love and respect for both God and the people around us. So let's not murder with our tongue. Let our hearts be pure.

CHAPTER 8
THE EIGHTH COMMANDMENT

Exodus 20:15: "You shall not steal."

The don't steal rule? That's not just about not going to jail! It's about being fair and understanding that other people worked hard for their stuff.
Imagine someone stealing your awesome new video game; that would totally hurt! Stealing messes things up for everyone, and it breaks trust. Being honest and respecting others' things builds a much better community, a place where you can actually trust people.

Stealing others' belongings, whether it's a candy bar or someone's ideas, is wrong. "You shall not steal." Stealing is bad, plain and simple. Even if it's just a tiny candy bar or a pencil from school, it's not right. Stealing is like totally violating someone's personal space and showing them you don't respect them or their things. Imagine how upset you'd be if someone swiped your phone or your favorite hoodie; that's exactly how the other person feels.

Ever been tempted to grab something that wasn't yours? Maybe you saw a twenty-dollar bill lying on the sidewalk, or a sweet pair of headphones left on a bus. What should you do? Simple, don't be a sneak! Turn it into a teacher, a parent, or someone who can help get it back to the owner. It's hard. Being honest and trustworthy makes you a better friend and a better person overall.

Cheating? That's stealing! I saw someone doing that online the other day, and it's so lame! It's not even fun if we cheat. When we cheat, we don't feel like we've accomplished anything. It's like, what's the point then? We feel way better about doing the right thing, even when it's hard. Being honest and trustworthy makes you a better friend and a better person overall. Cheating is missing the whole point of the game! It's like, we are worshipping winning more than the game itself, which is weird. And it's even worse when you say you believe in God, but then you're mean to people or cheat on a test. That's, like, the biggest lie ever! It's like saying you love pizza but then throwing it away. It doesn't make sense!

Matthew 6:19-20

"Do not lay up for yourselves treasures on earth, where moth and rust destroy and where thieves break in and steal; but lay up for yourselves treasures in heaven, where neither moth nor rust destroys and where thieves do not break in and steal."

Imagine you're playing a video game. You can spend all your time collecting fun weapons and power-ups, that's like earthly possessions. They're fun for a while, but when the game ends, they're gone. Instead, you can spend your time being kind, sharing your faith, and love. These treasures stay with you, even after you finish the game. That's what Jesus is talking about.

Jesus wants you to build a strong, happy life based on love and faith. It is important to let people know that Jesus died for their sins, took their punishment, and rose from the dead so they can have eternal life. This is the way they store their treasures in heaven. That's the real treasure, the one that lasts forever. So, while you enjoy the fun things in life, remember to invest in what truly matters: your relationships, your kindness, and your connection with God. That's where the lasting joy is found.

57

John 10:10

"The thief does not come except to steal, and to kill, and to destroy. I have come that they may have life, and that they may have it more abundantly."

Think of it like this: imagine a sneaky thief sneaking into your house. They only want to take things, your toys, your money, maybe even your TV! They're destructive, right? They might even hurt you if you catch them. That's what Jesus is saying the devil is like. He only wants to steal your happiness, kill your spirit, and destroy everything good in your life.

But Jesus is completely different! He's not here to take things away. He's here to give you life, a really awesome, amazing life filled with joy, hope, and love. He wants you to have life more abundantly, which means even more than you can imagine! It's like having a HUGE pile of your favorite candy, way, way more than you could ever eat! That's the kind of amazing life Jesus wants to give you. He wants you to have the best life possible, full of goodness and happiness. He wants to fill your life to overflowing!

1 Corinthians 6:10

"Nor thieves, nor covetous, nor drunkards, nor revilers, nor extortioners will inherit the kingdom of God."

That Bible verse says some pretty serious words! It means God's special place, heaven, isn't for people who act in certain ways. Let's break it down:

Thieves', stealing is wrong! It hurts other people and shows you don't respect their belongings. Think about how you'd feel if someone took something that was yours.

58

Covetous means being super jealous and wanting what others have, even if it's not fair to try to take it. It's about being greedy and unhappy with what you have. It's better to be thankful for what you do have.

Drunkards, drinking too much alcohol is dangerous and can really mess up your life and the lives of those around you. Alcohol causes people to make bad decisions and can even lead to health problems.

Revilers, this means being mean, insulting, and using harsh language to hurt others. Think about the power of kind words versus hurtful ones. Choose kindness!

Extortioners are people who use their power to force others to give them money or things they don't deserve. It's a form of bullying and unfairness.

The verse is basically saying that to be close to God, you need to be a good person who is kind, honest, and respects others and their things. It's a reminder to be our best selves. It's not about being perfect, because everyone makes mistakes. Still, it's about trying to be a good person and learning from our mistakes.

CHAPTER 9
THE NINTH COMMANDMENT

Exodus 20:15: "You shall not bear false witness against your neighbor."

The don't lie rule is about being truthful and trustworthy. Gossip and spreading rumors are like super-sized, mean lies. If you're always honest, people will learn to trust you more, which in turn leads to stronger friendships and relationships. Even small lies can mess things up in the long run. It's like building a house on sand; if you use lies as the foundation, it's gonna crumble.

Imagine a world where everyone is super nice and looks out for one another. That would be awesome! It would be a place where people help each other out, where you don't have to worry about getting picked on or hurt. Everyone's chill and friendly. It would just be a much better place to live.

61

Being honest builds trust. Not lying has to do with bigger things, like not copying someone else's homework; that's a major no-no! It means not being a tattletale or a gossip! Lying and spreading rumors are major relationship wreckers. Imagine how bummed you'd be if someone started a false story about you; it would totally hurt your feelings, right? This commandment means being careful with what you say. If you have a disagreement with someone, talk it out honestly and respectfully, instead of making things up or exaggerating the facts. Good communication means being fair and using your words to build people up, rather than tearing them down.

Have you ever heard that saying, "Sticks and stones may break my bones, but words will never hurt me?" That's totally a lie! Seriously, words can be way worse than a scraped knee. Gossiping or making up lies about someone can really hurt their feelings and wreck their friendships.

Think before you speak. Would you want someone to say that to you? It's not just what you say, but how you say it. Rolling your eyes or mumbling can be just as bad as a straight-up lie!

Have you ever played Telephone? You know, where you whisper something to the person next to you, and it gets passed down the line? By the time it gets to the end, it's totally different! Gossip starts with one little thing, maybe something someone said, saw, or heard someone else say, and then bam, it spreads like wildfire. Before you know it, it's a whole different story, and someone's feelings are totally crushed.
School can be a total gossip factory. Have you ever heard whispers in the hallway or seen people huddled together, giggling about someone? It's super contagious, and no one feels safe being themselves.

And here's the worst part: sometimes, the person who started the gossip doesn't even realize how much damage they've done. They might have just meant to share a little fun fact, but their fun fact became someone else's nightmare. That's why it's important to think before you speak, and to remember that even a tiny little seed of a lie can grow into a huge, thorny bush that hurts a lot of people. Being honest and kind is way better and way more fun!

Even if someone says something mean or spreads a rumor, try to forgive them. It doesn't mean what they did was okay, but holding onto anger just makes you feel bad. Praying can really help with that. Letting go is the best way to move on and feel better.

Following God's rules isn't just about following a list; it's about being a good person. It's about being kind, respectful, and responsible. When you do good things, it's not just good for God, it's good for everyone, making the world a safer and happier place. It's a journey, not a race, so keep trying your best to be a good person, and ask for help when you need it! Let's all spread kindness, truth, and love!

63

And by the way, being a good person does not get you to heaven. Being a good person is like training for a marathon; it helps you grow and become stronger, and it's a really important part of life. It teaches us to walk in love, to treat others with kindness and respect, and to make the world a better place. But getting to heaven isn't about earning points for good deeds. It's like getting a really amazing gift.

What gets you to heaven is a gift, the amazing gift of Jesus' sacrifice on the cross. Imagine this: you've done something wrong, something really big, and you're facing a huge punishment. Someone else, someone you don't even know, steps in and takes that punishment for you, even though they didn't do anything wrong. That's what Jesus did. When He was beaten and crucified, He allowed that to happen because He loves you so much. He wants to be with you, not just for a little while, but eternally, forever.

64

If He did not die on the cross, was buried, and rose from the dead, we would still be separated from God. He says, "He who believes that I am the Son of God and died for them," that's the key. It's about trusting in Him and what He did for you. It's about accepting that gift of love and forgiveness. It's not about being perfect; it's about believing in the amazing love Jesus has for you. Think of it as accepting a super cool present that someone gave you; you don't have to earn it, you just have to open it and enjoy it!

65

CHAPTER 10
THE TENTH COMMANDMENT

Exodus 20:15: "You shall not covet your neighbor's house; you shall not covet your neighbor's wife, nor his male servant, nor his female servant, nor his ox, nor his donkey, nor anything that is your neighbor's."

Think about the "Ten Commandments." The tenth one says, "Don't be jealous of what others have." It's not just about wanting someone else's stuff; it's about wanting it so badly that it makes you obsessed. It makes you envious, grumpy, and might even make you lie or cheat, manipulate, or control to get it. It's way better to be happy with what you've have and remember everyone has neat things about them.

For young people, coveting can look different. Maybe you're super jealous of your friend's awesome new video game, or you wish you got as much attention as someone else. Maybe you even wish you had a different family or a better life. But jealousy makes you unhappy because you're focusing on what you don't have, not what you do have.

Imagine Sarah and Emily. Sarah has a sweet new bike, and Emily doesn't. If Emily's jealous, she might get mad at Sarah, start rumors, or even try to mess up Sarah's bike! But if Emily isn't jealous, she might say, "Wow, that's a fun bike!" She may ask Sarah about it or even save up her allowance to get her own bike. Jealousy can make you do sneaky things. A kid might steal a friend's game or lie to their parents to get one. Lying ruins trust and friendships, and it doesn't even make you happy! Real happiness comes from being thankful for what you have and being nice to others.

Let's talk about real-life situations where this advice actually matters. Like, if your best friend tells you a huge secret, don't blab it to everyone! That's a major betrayal. Be there for them, listen, and offer a shoulder to cry on or a high-five, depending on the situation!

And if you see someone getting picked on, seriously, don't just stand there like a statue! Step in and help. Even if it's just saying, "Hey, leave them alone!" It makes a difference. Being a bystander is almost as bad as being the bully.

Ever get super jealous of someone's awesome new phone or whatever? Instead of being upset about what you don't have, think about what you do have. Maybe you're amazing at drawing, or a total whiz at video games, or a fantastic baker. Focus on your stuff and use your talents to help others; that's way more satisfying than any gadget. Your skills, whatever they are, are awesome, and you should share them. That's way better than having a bunch of things.

Sharing is where it's at! Sharing games, books, and even just hanging out shows you respect others and makes your friendships even stronger. It's all about being a good friend, not about who has the best things. When you share, you're not just giving someone something; you're making your friendship way more awesome! Think of it as friendship glue!

68

Imagine how much better things would be if we all celebrated each other's wins instead of feeling bummed when someone else does well. That's what the Golden Rule is all about, treating others how you want to be treated. It's like cheering on your friend's sports team, even if they're playing against your favorite team; it's all about supporting your friends.

Being honest and true to yourself and to other people, trust you more, and that makes everything way more fun and easier. It's kind of like leveling up in a video game, honesty and kindness are your best power-ups!

CHAPTER 11
THE FINAL COMMANDMENT

Mark 12: 30-31, 33 "30 And you shall love the Lord your God with all your heart, with all your soul, with all your mind, and with all your strength.' This is the first commandment. 31 And the second, like it, is this: 'You shall love your neighbor as yourself.' There is no other commandment greater than these."

How do you love God with all your heart if you cannot see Him? How do you know He is there? How do you find Him? How do you love Him with all your heart, soul, mind, and strength? That's, like, way more than just saying you love Him. Being friends with Jesus is like having a secret, awesome best friend who's always there for you. It's great to want to love God, but how do you love someone you can't see? Remember these images at the beginning of this book?

God loves us so much that He became a human just for us. He was

beaten and died on the cross to pay for our sins. The blood that He shed on the cross erases our sins as if our sins were never there. God is holy and hates sin. He had to erase our sins so He could be with us in heaven forever. He forgave us because He loves us and wants a relationship with us.

After He was hung on the cross, Jesus went back up to

heaven, on the third day, and overcame death for all who believe in Him. Now He sits in glory beside the Father. He promises that He will return so everyone can see how beautiful He is when He **comes back.**

71

Our relationship with Jesus depends completely on His grace. He is sinless. He died for us, on the cross, so that we could be with Him. He sent the Holy Spirit, who makes it possible for us to show God how much we love Him. The Holy Spirit guides, strengthens, and comforts us.

After Jesus died and was raised up to heaven, He sent His Holy Spirit to take care of us. Our life with Jesus depends completely on His acting the way God wants us to. We are a part of Him. God sees us as holy because Jesus took our sins on the cross. The Holy Spirit guides us, strengthens, and comforts us when we are sad or scared. He blesses us with peace and hope and promises that He will never leave us.

Therefore, the Spirit of Jesus is with us at all times. He knows where we are and what we are doing. He is helping us. He is living in us. Imagine it's like having a super-powered best friend who's always there, even when you can't see him! He loves us because we believe He is there, and we believe that He is the Son of God. He helps us even when we mess up. His love is not something we earn; it's a gift.

72

So, how do you love Jesus, whom you can't see? You can sing worship songs to Him. He loves our singing. You can play music for Him.

Praying to Him is very special. When we pray, and actually mean it with our whole heart, it is very important. Rushing through prayer because you want to hang with friends is not praying with your whole heart. He hears us. He answers our prayers the way He wants to. Remember, He is guiding us. When we pray, we are showing Him that we believe in Him and we have faith in Him.

Reading His Bible as often as we can is another way to get to know Jesus. Being obedient to His word makes Him very happy and brings us closer to Him. Sin keeps us far away from Him.

Another thing God loves is when we talk to Him. Yes, talking to Him just like you talk with a friend, like He is right in the room with you. All these things help us to know Jesus and to love Him more and more every day.

Worshipping Him by singing to Him, praying to Him, reading His Bible, and talking to Him are the ways we get to know Him. This is how we have a personal relationship with our amazing God of love. This is loving God with all your heart, with all your soul, with all your mind, and with all your strength.

73

Now, He also wants us to love our neighbor as ourselves. What did Jesus really mean when He used the word "neighbor?" To Jesus, "neighbor" means everyone we come into contact with.

We love our own families a lot, but we should love God more than our family or anyone. He gave us our family. We are supposed to love our friends, brothers, and sisters in Christ, and all people, no matter what nationality they are or the religion they believe in. We are even supposed to love our enemies.

How does Jesus want us to love others? Jesus showed love to others by serving people, being humble, showing mercy, compassion, and sacrificing the things He liked, even when it was not easy or fun for Him. Jesus gave us everything, and He wants us to give to others. If you really love Jesus, you'll want to do good because you want to please Him.

The best way to love others is to follow the example Jesus left us in the Bible. He helped people to understand the gospel that He died for our sins, rose from the dead, and is alive in heaven. He taught us this, so anyone in the world can go to heaven if they believe it. He taught us how to forgive, showed us how to confess our sins to each other, to be sorry for our sins, and change our ways to good ways. He wants us to do all these things.

It's like a big circle. You love God, and God helps you love other people, and then loving other people makes you feel good, which makes you want to love God even more. It's kind of a win-win-win thing, I guess. Plus, it makes the world a way better place. No more unhappy people everywhere! We need to love and be like Jesus. The commandments that God gave us are all about His love for us.

Imagine a world where everyone smiles, not just because they have to, but because they feel happy. That's the kind of world the Tween Commandments help us build! Think of them less like strict rules and more like super-secret codes for a happier life. They're not about getting in trouble; they're about unlocking amazing things inside yourself, like bravery, confidence, and the power to make a real difference.

These commandments aren't about being perfect, because no one is. It's about trying your best, even when it's hard. Maybe you

75

accidentally say something mean. The important thing is to apologize and learn from it. It's like learning to ride a bike; you'll fall sometimes, but you get back up and keep trying. Each time you choose kindness, honesty, or respect, you're building up your inner strength, like adding another brick to a magnificent castle of goodness!

The stories in this book have shown you how these commandments work in real life, with characters who face challenges just like you. You'll see how making the right choices, even when it's tough, leads to amazing adventures and strong friendships.

Remember, being kind isn't just about being nice; it's about showing empathy, understanding how other people feel, and lending a helping hand. Honesty isn't just about not lying; it's about being truthful even when it's difficult. And respect isn't just about manners; it's about valuing yourself and everyone around you, recognizing their unique worth.

The book you just read is a journey of discovery. Now you have a chance to explore what it truly means to live a life filled with love, faith, and happiness. You learned how to find your superpower – the power to make the world a brighter, kinder place, one good deed at a time. So let your adventures begin! And don't forget to share the secret superpower of happiness with everyone you know!

Do you love the Lord your God with all your heart, with all your soul, and with all your mind? Do you love others as yourself?

Do you love?

1 John 4: 7-8 NKJV 7 Beloved, let us love one another, for love is of God; and everyone who loves is born of God and knows God. 8 He who does not love does not know God, for God is love.

Have you given your life to Jesus?
If you wish, this is all you need to do.

Open your heart to the Lord Jesus, surrender your life, and believe that He is the Son of God. Invite Jesus into your life and ask for forgiveness of your sins, as well as His guidance.

Out loud say, I acknowledge you, Jesus, as my Savior and Lord. I thank you, Jesus, for Your sacrifice on the cross and for taking my punishment. Please shape me into the person You want me to be.